MW00885779

FROM THE DARKNESS TO THE LIGHT

Ildiko Eva Szombathy

AuthorHouse™ LLC
1663 Liberty Drive
Bloomington, IN 47403
www.authorhouse.com
Phone: 1-800-839-8640

Published by AuthorHouse 09/25/2014

ISBN: 978-1-4389-7559-7 (sc)

This book is printed on acid-free paper.

DEDICATION

To my dear children Bela Jr. and Melinda, my grandchildren Viktoria, Kristina, Jaime Jr. and the generations to come.

ACKNOWLEDGMENTS

I would like to thank my daughter Melinda and her husband Jaime, my son Bela Jr. and his wife Terry for actively participating in translating and carrying out the manuscript.

Contents

PROLOGUE

I have written two books about my life. The first book reflects my views of living in the darkness of communism and the transition into the light of freedom.

All the characters in the story are authentic and the events are real.

Even now, after twenty-three years of freedom, it is emotionally difficult to retrieve from my memory the miserable life of a child who was deprived of her parents.

Furthermore, the unjust events exerted onto me and my innocent family and the impact on our integrity as human beings for many years to come.

With this book, I would also like to promote freedom of religion and enhance patriotism.

For the protection of the surviving characters, some details of events were withheld.

CHAPTER 1

The Child was Born

"Those who did not agree with the new order were marked for life."

THE YEAR WAS 1945; WORLD WAR II HAD ENDED IN HUNGARY, Romania, and Transylvania. The Russians had won, even though they did not have good battle plans or sophisticated combat tactics. They won thanks to the high military outcomes of the United States of America, whose main goal was to declare war on Japan for attacking Pearl Harbor - Hawaii, and later, to crush dictator, Hitler. The Russians cared little for human life; the only thing they cared about was winning this terrible war. The Russian army was known for stealing money and gold from the citizens of the conquered countries. They raped the women, and executed their husbands if they came to the defense of their wives. To avoid being molested by the soldiers, young Hungarian girls would try to alter their appearance by rubbing black ash on their faces and bodies, and they wore old, raggedy clothes.

The last battle of World War II on Hungarian soil was between the Russian and German armies. This battle was fought in Budapest, the capital of Hungary. The Russians had trapped the Germans in the

Hungarian king's castle district, which was beautiful and massive. It consisted of streets lined with historic homes and churches. Budapest, the capital, is actually two cities: Buda (the older city) and Pest (the modern one) are connected together with several bridges that span the Danube River. God blessed the Hungarian capital with its natural beauty. Houses made of metal and concrete stood tall in the castle district.

Most of Transylvania's high-class civilians spent their wartime in these houses, huddled in the basements with their relatives who sheltered them. They thought it would be safer to live in the country's capital during the war. They could not have been more mistaken. Budapest was heavily bombed; the only buildings still standing were the ones built of steel and concrete. As the battle raged on between the German and Russian armies, the terrified Hungarian civilians—called refugees—waited together in fear. The ground shook from exploding bombs, they covered their ears to muffle the sound of the battle. They prayed that they and their loved ones would survive. As the last remnants of the Hungarian regal castle district was bombed to the ground, the German army finally surrendered. On a nearby street, only one house was still standing. This house was damaged by gunfire and bombs. A woman named Korina (the mother of the writer) was hiding with her relatives and friends. Korina's husband was away fighting in the war. All men under the age of fifty were drafted. It was mandatory to fight.

Transylvania and the Romanian states also underwent smaller attacks, but the Romanian states put down their weapons and let the enemy through Transylvania toward Budapest. The Romanian king, Karol, had been dethroned and exiled, and the country was awaiting the new order.

Transylvania was a region where Hungarians had lived since the Huns (what they called the Hungarians in the old days) occupied the land in the Carpathian Basin under their "good King Attila"during the 5th Century A.D. The people who lived in Transylvania were called Transylvanians (Szekely) settled at the pillar of the Harghita mountain, since the ancient King Attila's son, prince Csaba reached the southwest side of the Carpathian Mountains. To the east and south of the Carpathians stood the Romanian principalities developed between the 13th and 14th centuries. On many occasions, the Romanian armies had invaded Transylvania, but these battles never lasted long. The Hungarians always pushed them back.

After the Trianon Treaty was signed in 1920, the Romanians received the whole country of Transylvania without fighting.

After the brief history of this region; let's get back to the Transylvanian refugees who were now getting ready to go back home. The people who escaped from Transylvania to Budapest, to avoid the Russian armies, now lost almost everything. Some lost their homes, but all lost animals, buggies, and food during the war. They now turned back to their homes in Transylvania with fear in their hearts. The end of the Second World War in Russia's favor was the onset of communism. They were afraid of what was going to happen to those who did not agree with the Russian government and did not want to live under a communist regime.

Korina Szombathy—the daughter of Zoltan Forro and Korina Zathureczky – was raised by her uncle, Kalman Zathureczky, the Three County Judge. Korina was nurtured by a nanny, since her uncle Kalman did not have a wife or children. Gabor Szombathy was Korina's husband. The Zathureczky-Forro, and Szombathy-Bartha families were old nobility and were well known in Transylvania. Kalman, Korina's uncle, died during the war. Gabor and his brothers were held in war prisons, even though the war had ended. All four families owned a lot of land, forests, houses, farms, and livestock.

Korina was on her way to Transylvania, to her hometown, Ajta. Ajta is a bigger village at the foot of the Carpathian Mountains. This is where her property was before the war began. If Korina had any idea what her future would bring, she would never have returned home. What was her journey back to Ajta like? Korina was apprehensive. She was worried about her family, who did not agree with the communist regime. Those who did not agree with the new order were marked for life.

Gabor and Korina on the streets of Brasso - Transylvania.

In those days, traveling from Budapest to Transylvania by horse and buggy took about two weeks. Korina took the train a few days after the war ended, when train transportation was available again. On the way, she saw the destruction of her homeland. Houses and buildings were riddled with holes from gunfire and bombs, and most were completely destroyed. Confused and wounded animals were wandering the streets, looking for food and a place to go. Korina tried not to look at the dead bodies left lying on the side of the road. And then she encountered the homeless and the injured, some missing limbs, some missing an eye. All were starving. They would hold out their scarred arms and beg for food from any stranger they saw. The Russian soldiers did not have enough food, so they would search the refugees and confiscate any they found. She had no food to feed herself, so she could give them nothing. How her heart cried for them. When she tried to sleep, her exhausted mind would replay all the horror she had witnessed. She saw the fearful faces of the women who tried to hide behind ash-smeared bodies and raggedy clothes, hoping to go unnoticed by the soldiers. She saw husbands murdered by these same soldiers when they tried to protect their women from being raped. She dreamed of the last goodbye to her husband before he went off to war.

Relieved that she had finally made it home to Ajta, Korina was shocked to see that all her fine china was smashed to pieces and had been scattered on the road. When she arrived at her house, she was dismayed to see all the windows gone and the door wide open. The soldiers and looters had ransacked her home, taken what they wanted, and destroyed the rest. The farm machinery was gone; livestock had been taken or had wandered away; even the wheat had disappeared from the back barn. They were left with nothing. Ida, the elderly nanny who was left to care for the house during the war, was an eyewitness to the destruction and theft. Korina and her husband would have to replace everything; thank goodness she had the foresight to hide some money in the back yard, under the big tree.

As mentioned before, Gabor, Korina's husband, was captured and held prisoner during the war. Korina had no news of him and had no idea what had happened. One day long after the war ended Gabor did return home. His hands and feet were half frozen, but he was glad to be home and thankful his wife was well. At this time, socialism was well on its way. Socialism is the pre-phase of communism. During this phase, people's land, animals, money, farming equipment, and anything else of value was taken from them. In every town, collectivism began. This meant that everything became common property; this process was called *equalization,* or *given by free will.* There were people who did not like to work, or drank their money away; these people liked this way of thinking. But to most honest and hard-working ones, this was an unjust way of life. The working people were paid just enough to get by, and any profit was the property of the government.

Lenin was the inventor of communism, the continuation of the Marx and Engels theory. Stalin brought to reality their idealism in Russia, which believed that communism denies the existence of God, and persecutes everyone who does not uphold these views. This did not stop on Russian territory. Stalin and the Communist Party wanted to spread it throughout the world. Communism was "the red epidemic." This is what people called the regime. Everyone was afraid to speak against this terror. They were afraid of what would happen to themselves as well as their families. In those days, it was common for people to disappear and never be seen or heard from again. This was the time when the Hungarian Holy Crown and the Coronation Regalia needed to be protected from invaders. The United States of America guarded the Hungarian Royal Treasures for thirty years in Kentucky, therefore the Hungarian nation is forever grateful. In 1978, after the situation stabilized in Hungary, President Carter returned the treasures. Today they can be admired in the Hungarian National Museum in Budapest.

Gabor and Korina had a beautiful house, acres of land, a lot of livestock, and farming equipment which they inherited. Their ancestors were wealthy nobles. Many years back, tradition had it that the king rewarded his brave soldiers who fought well for their king and country with land, money, and the title of "noble." This is where Gabor and Korina's wealth came from. Their family tree dates back to the 1250s, when the old Latin language was still widely used, and is recorded in old family documents passed down through the generations.

The ancient noble Beczkoi Szombathy family's Coat-of-arms.

Explanation of the crest: A gold lion on blue field holding a sword. The helmet above the shield is topped by a five pointed crown. The crown in the crest signifies the status of the possessor as a defender of his country and king. The decoration of the helmet and the cover of the shield are gold-red on the right side and silver-blue on the left. The arm with the sword above the crown is a symbolic representation of its country's protector.

The ancient noble Szombathy family was documented in Latin as Tirna, Tyrnavia, Tyrnaviensis.

The first decedent Gregorius Tirna was commander of Pozsony County-Hungary in 1250. Andreas de Tirna was a catholic priest in 1313. The Tirnas built a chapel inside the Saint Stephen Cathedral in Vienna-Austria during 1395. The chapel is the burial place of Prince Eugene of Savoy; it is also where the funeral of Mozart was held. This chapel is still known as Tyrna – Kapelle or Chapel of the Cross.

Ladislaus de Tirna served as general of King Albert between 1437-1442.

Martinus de Tyrnavia was the advisor of King Louis II (the brave king who died in the Battle of Mohacs in 1526), between 1517-1527.

Gergely Szombathy/Gregorius Tyrnaviensis the first ancestor with a hungarian name, was major of Szepes County-Hungary between 1567-1604.

The updated Szombathy family tree is in Ildiko's possession thanks to her great-great grandfather Dr. Szombathy Ignacz. He gathered the necessary documents, and in 1892 wrote the first book in Hungarian about the two branches of the Szombathy family, Tirnai and Beczkoi. Ildiko and her family belong to the Beczkoi branch, which was recently updated by Agnes Ottahal, great-great granddaughter of Agnes Szombathy. The title of nobility Beczkoi is coming from the city of Beczko , where Gyorgy (George) Szombathy and his family resided in the 1500-1600s, to escape the destruction of the Turkish occupancy. See "Disaster of Mohacs", 1526. The Tirnai branch became extinct in the 1600s.

All of their money and most of their land and animals were taken by the government. They were left with the house, a little land to work, and a few animals to live off of. Gabor and Korina knew that the hard times were not over yet. They sensed that there was more to come as communism spread throughout the country. They went to sleep every night with fear in their hearts, worrying about what the next day would bring.

In this uncertain and scary period of their lives, God gave them a reason to believe and to live. In August of 1946, after eleven years of marriage, they were blessed with a daughter. The couple was thrilled and named her Ildiko. The Szombathy-Bartha and the Zathureczky-

Forro families were filled with happiness and celebrated the birth of Ildiko. In these hard times, Gabor and Korina's child brought joy and meaning to their lives. They felt that the three of them, along with Ida the nanny, could start a new life together.

The Szombathy family before deportation.

Ildiko sitting on her mother's lap having a good time enjoying her family's attention.

CHAPTER 2

Their Worst Fear Comes True

"Two and a half years after Ildiko was born, their worst fear came true."

GABOR AND KORINA WORKED EVERY DAY FROM MORNING UNTIL evening. Ida Mama took care of baby Ildiko. As mentioned before, Ida Mama was once Korina's nanny as well. She was also the housekeeper of Korina's uncle Kalman. When Kalman adopted Korina, Ida helped raise her, and she loved her as if she were her own child. During her marriage Ida gave birth to nine children, all died; some right after birth, others in their very early childhood. Because Ida was getting older, Korina did not dismiss her from the family when she married. Both Korina and her husband treated Ida as if she were their own mother.

Two and a half years after Ildiko was born, their worst fear came true. One night, in March of 1949, the baby was restless and crying, and she would not fall asleep. They tried to comfort her but nothing soothed her; she cried and cried. I suppose it's true when they say that children can sense danger. At midnight, there was loud pounding at the door and windows. Voices were shouting to open up at once. Gabor jumped out of the bed and raced to open the door. Soldiers and unknown men in plain clothes pushed their way in and surrounded both Gabor and Korina. At gunpoint, they shouted at them as if they were criminals. They gave them only ten minutes to dress and gather a few belongings, all the while shouting "Down with the rotten capitalist!" They demanded jewelry, gold, or anything else of value. Korina, hearing this, hid some money in a wastebasket, hoping the neighbor lady would find it and be able to use it. The soldiers asked Gabor how much money he had. Gabor, being an honest man, told them the exact amount. Korina then had to get the money and give them all of it.

Ida Mama held Ildiko in her arms. The child was quiet, her eyes bright with fear in the presence of these shouting men. Ildiko held on tighter and tighter to Ida's neck. The ten minutes ended quickly and it was time to leave. One of the leaders told Ida that her time of serving was over and she was free to go wherever she wanted. Ida answered, "I was with them through good times, and I will stay with them through the bad times." The family was loaded into the truck that was waiting in front of the house. On the truck, they found Gabor's brother Gyula and his wife, Korina's cousin Benke Laci, among other relatives and friends. Some of them were still wearing their nightclothes, were not given the chance to pack any belongings. Armed guards surrounded them. The men were handcuffed. The only voices heard were the children asking, "Mommy, where are we going?" and the whispered response of "I don't know, sweetheart. Be quiet now." Everyone was thinking the same thing: They thought they were on the way to Siberia, a place from where no one returns. They prayed that God would keep them safe. Why was this happening to them? What did they do wrong? Who convicted them? There were no answers to their questions; they were met with silence and scorn. The prisoners did not believe in communism and did not want to become communists; this was their only crime. Because of this, the government wanted to get rid of them. It stoled their money and stripped them of everything they owned. They were forced to work in hard labor camps with just enough food to keep them alive. This was how they were forced to build the communist country stronger.

As the truck drove away, the prisoners grew more fearful. The guards made it impossible to look out and see the surroundings. After a four-hour drive, the truck finally came to a stop. They had reached their first destination, a city in the county of Kovaszna named Saintgeorge (Szentgyorgy). Once there, the soldiers commanded everyone off the truck. The prisoners were herded into the police station where they joined sixty-five other people who were there awaiting orders. After what seemed like hours, they were all placed in a large house. This house had already gone through the naturalizing process, which meant, that it was taken from the owners. In the morning, forced labor started at rifle point. Day after day, from four o'clock in the morning until the sun went down, they cleaned the pastures and cultivated the land. Sometime later, some of the prisoners were taken to work in a nearby glass factory. No matter where they worked, talking was forbidden. Both men and women had armed guards watching them wherever they went.

Korina was afraid they would be taken to a much further destination. One night, the guard sold Korina's wedding ring and got drunk off the money. After he passed out, Korina sneaked Ida and Ildiko out of the house and ran to the house next door. She begged the people who lived there to take her daughter and the nanny to her mother's house in Besenyo. Besenyo was a small village in Transylvania at the southwest corner of the Carpathian Mountains. It was sometimes referred to as the "Hidden Village," because the forests owned by Korina's father surrounded it. Korina was convinced that this was the only way she could save her daughter from what was to come. In the morning, the new guard was unconcerned with the disappearance of the old lady and baby; they could not be put to work anyway. Since phone calls and letter were not a privilege, Gabor and Korina would wonder for more than five years if their child and nanny had made it to safety, or if they were still alive.

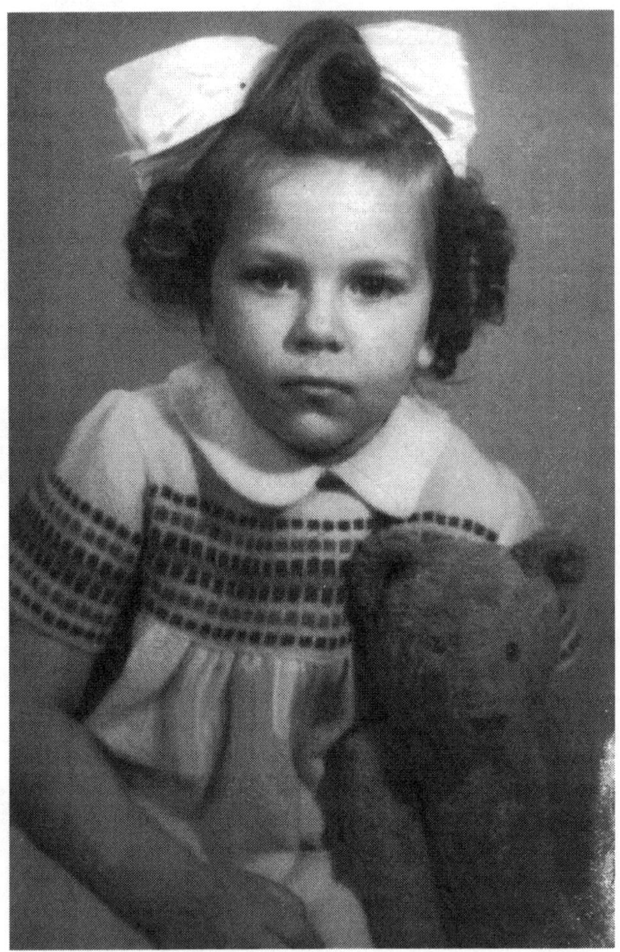

Three-year-old Ildiko after the deportation of her parents.

CHAPTER 3

Life in the Forced Labor Camp

"In this place the prisoners reaped rice in the water that came up to their knees."

Six months slowly passed. One night, the prisoners were moved again. The armed military guards shoved the women and kicked the men into train boxcars used for animal transportation. It was very quiet; everyone was exhausted and the air was heavy with fear. After a while, the train stopped. The guards started to load more people into the already overcrowded boxcars. Some of the men quietly asked the newcomers what city this was. That was how Gabor and Korina found out they were now in Brasso, which was another big city in Transylvania. Once everyone was loaded, the guards ordered silence. After a long ride, they were in one of the oldest and poorest regions of Romania: the city of Cerna Voda, Macin district in the Galati region. This is located southeast of the Carpathian Mountains. In this place, the prisoners reaped rice in water that came up to their knees. One day, Korina cut her finger on a rusty sickle. She became very ill of blood poisoning. Her finger was infected and she was suffering from a high fever that would not break. There was no doctor or medical facility in the area. Both Korina and the guards knew that if she did not get medical attention soon, she would die. One of the guards took her to the closest hospital in Braila, a port city. After the doctors examined Korina, the guard insisted on taking her back to the labor camp right away, but the doctor wouldn't allow it. With the care at the hospital, Korina was able to recover in a week's time.

Before Christmas, they were again transported, this time by boat, down the Danube to a farm called Puiernitza located in the same county as the labor camp. This was a thorny, burned-out area where not even grass would grow. This labor camp had long wooden buildings, each house held thirty-five people. Each person was given a wooden bed and one blanket. The prisoners had to stand in line every day for their meal, which consisted of a small bowl of soup and a little cornmeal or barley. This was just enough food to keep them from dying of starvation. In this camp, the guards were Romanian communists who called the prisoners *bozgor* ("homeless"). In Romanian, these and similar words were used often across the country as communism was in its development.

In the morning, while standing in line, the prisoners received their assignment for the day. This was an animal farm; Korina was assigned to care for twelve cows and one calf. She had to clean their stalls, feed them, and milk them three times a day. This was an enormous task for one woman. In order to ease her burden, Korina named each cow after a family member and some close friends. She named the calf after someone she adored and who was always close to her heart—her daughter, Ildiko. While Korina was struggling with the cows, her husband Gabor and some of the other men were sent to Braila. Here, they were constructing agricultural buildings and brought food back to the camp for the animals.

The following spring, the guards came one night and took Gabor away in shackles. No one but the guards knew his destination. He was transported to Bekasi (*Bicaz* in Romanian) Prison; at that time, it was one of the largest in the country. More manpower was needed for the construction of the water power station, which later would supply many Romanian cities with electricity. In this prison, he was held with other political prisoners, murderers, and other criminals, and was forced to work in striped prison garb. The tremendous physical labor and poor food slowly made Gabor very sick to his stomach, and he began to pass blood. Refusing to eat, he started a hunger strike. He thought that this way, the guards would take him before the court, so he could be informed of the charges he was being held on. The hunger strike was met with no result.

It took Gabor five years to get his wish, to stand before a court of justice. This happened as a result of pressure exerted for many years on the Supreme Court of Romania by the population of their village, Ajta. These loyal people sent hundreds of letters signed by the residents from the majority of the regions of Transylvania, explaining the couple's goodness and thoughtfulness to everyone, especially the poor. The couple had thirteen godchildren in their village, and Gabor made sure that all of them received everything they needed. There was not a single person who went to Gabor for something and was turned away. He gave what he could when he could, and people loved and respected him for it. That was his character and that was the way he lived.

At the trial, he found out that he was charged with being an enemy of communism, and that such a person did not *deserve* freedom. But God's mercy is endless. He listened to the prayers of Gabor's daughter, family, and friends, and Gabor regained his freedom. By this time, he was so ill that they had no use for him; he could no longer work. Gyula, Gabor's brother, died this way in prison, leaving behind a wife and two small children, Aranka and Erzso.

Gabor left the prison in 1954. The only thing he was given was a train ticket to his brother Laci's house. Laci and his family resided in Borosnyo, Transylvania. They took care of Gabor and Korina's most precious and only wealth, their daughter Ildiko. The little girl lived with her grandparents until she reached school age. Since there was no school in Besenyo, she had no choice but to go live with her uncle and his family.

CHAPTER 4

From Protective Wings to "Real Life"

"The little girl was silent; huge tears ran down her sad face."

ILDIKO'S STORY CONTINUES ON THE NIGHT WHEN HER MOTHER KORINA had the foresight to sneak her out of the first camp in Saintgeorge (Szentgyorgy) and beg the nearby neighbors to take her child and the nanny to safety. Those wonderful people kept their promise and took both child and nanny to Besenyo. In Besenyo, they lived with the family of Ildiko's maternal grandmother, Aunt Eva, and her uncle. Grandma had a large house; there was room for everyone. Ildiko and Ida even had their own room. The hateful communists had left the house and the surrounding yard in the ownership of Korina's mother, but they took the rest of the land, which included forests and orchards. The farm animals all became community property called "collective" except for one cow. Life was hard for the family, but they accepted Ildiko and Ida into their home and raised the little girl with lots of love, but in her heart something was still missing. She craved the love of her mother and father and missed them very much. Every night, when she went to bed, she prayed for her parents to return.

Her life was simple in this village. Ida took care of Ildiko's daily needs and Grandma cooked the best chicken paprikas for her. There wasn't much food, just what they could grow in the back yard, and a few chickens, a pig, and a cow. Sometime later, they were forced to sell the cow, because they had no food to feed it and couldn't afford to buy any. The communists made them pay taxes on food and money.

Most of the time, Ildiko played by herself. There were not many children who lived around them, and she was not allowed to go to other children's houses, because the adults feared for her safety. She played in the front yard, where Grandma had managed to grow some flowers, including violets, a yellow rose bush, and a white berry bush. Ildiko would often nap in the shade of the berry bush. There was peace and quiet in the front yard. She liked that. Her favorite thing to do was to go into the forest and pick mushrooms; it was fun and helped feed the family. One afternoon, while picking mushrooms with Aunt Eva, they stumbled upon a beautiful place in the middle of the forest, in the south west Carpathians. It was a meadow where the ground was covered in red from the little wild strawberries that grew there. This beautiful field became Ildiko's favorite place to go. In one of the forests, there was a place where arthritis-healing mineral water flowed from the ground. Many people regained their health by soaking and bathing in these springs. This area of the Carpathians is widely known for the healing power of these mineral-water springs.

At the house, in the back yard, there were many different kinds of fruit trees. Ildiko had two favorites. One produced little red apples and the other grew low and parallel to the ground, making it the perfect climbing tree.

Every evening when Ildiko went to bed, she sucked her thumb. Everyone told her that it was a bad habit and she should try to quit doing it. One night, they put paprika and black pepper on her thumb to help her break the habit. It didn't work. She still sucked her thumb. The next day, Aunt Eva showed Ildiko a beautiful three-strand coral pearl necklace and said she could have it if she stopped sucking her thumb. She really liked the necklace and struggled to stop. The first few nights were the hardest. She had trouble falling asleep. But after that, each night became easier, and she finally succeeded. Ildiko was very proud of herself. The necklace was hers. How she adored that necklace; she had never owned anything more beautiful.

A week went by, and visitors came to the neighbor's house. They had a daughter who was a couple of years older than Ildiko. She wanted to play with the girl and thought she would impress her by wearing the beautiful coral necklace. As they were playing, the girl asked to wear the necklace just for the night and she would return it in the morning. Ildiko agreed. The next morning, the family was gone. They had left that same night. Ildiko was very upset; her most prized possession was gone. She cried for a time, but what bothered her the most was that she had been deceived.

The years went by slowly. Ildiko was almost five years old, and it was time for her to leave Besenyo in order to start school. She had to say goodbye to her grandparents, aunt, and uncle, who were the only family she knew. She would miss them and the flowers, the little red apple tree, and the climbing tree. The little girl was silent; huge tears ran down her sad face. It felt as if she had been abducted again. They packed her up and a horse-drawn wagon took her to Borosnyo to her uncle Laci's house. The owner of this wagon was their Russian neighbor, who fell in love with a Hungarian woman during the war. They married and started a life together in Besenyo. Ildiko did not know her uncle Laci or his family, but hoped that they would like her. Ida had to stay behind in Besenyo, because Ildiko's uncle had a big family, and could not provide for both of them. This was very painful for Ildiko. Ida had been with her since birth and was the only one consistently taking care of her throughout her life. She loved her dearly.

Laci and his family were nice to Ildiko, but were very strict. They had two sons, Pista and Gabi. Laci's mother-in-law also lived with them. Ildiko tried to behave the best she could and tried to care for herself so she would not be a burden on them. Laci was also called *kulak* ("against communism") and *burzsuly* ("rotten capitalist"), and the system's representatives made his life as hard as possible. They took over most of his land, animals, money, and wagons to the collective. Laci had a big stone house, but he did not have enough wood to keep it warm in the winter. Many times, the whole family went to bed in a freezing cold house. Food was a problem as well. Most of the time, vegetable soup was the only thing the family had for dinner. When chicken was available, they only cooked it on Sundays.

While living with her uncle and his family in Borosnyo.

CHAPTER 5

Discrimination and Disappointment

"She was called kizsakmanyolo (exploiter)."

Ildiko turned five years old in August of 1951. September was right around the corner. It was time for her to start kindergarten. She was frustrated and afraid when Anna, Laci's wife, took her to school. They were late. Anna couldn't come home earlier from working on the field, where she had been since four o'clock that morning. There were very few wristwatches at that time, and they did not own one. When they arrived a few minutes after nine o'clock, everybody was angry with the little girl. The children made fun of her by singing the blame song: "You were lazy, you slept late, and you didn't learn anything nice today." All the children pulled away from her. Ildiko sat by herself for four hours every day while she was in kindergarten. The teacher did not care, because she considered her to be an enemy of the communist system. Communists occupied positions paid by the state; other people were dismissed. This was the way Ildiko's cousin Aranka lost her job. Aranka was a geography teacher and died at the age of thirty-nine of a brain tumor. She left behind a husband with two little girls, Aniko and Kati.

Ildiko didn't want to go to kindergarten, but it was a must. She did not make any friends the whole year. No one wanted to be her friend. Children are innocent at that age; they know only what they are taught. In those days, children were taught at home not to be friends with people like Ildiko, whose family did not believe in the new system. She was called *kizsakmanyolo* ("exploiter"). Other children just followed the majority. Some simply didn't want to get in trouble during that unstable time and were afraid to be close with her. People were so afraid that even old friends did not greet Laci and his family when they ran into them on the street.

In 1953, Ildiko started first grade with the same children from kindergarten. She was sad and hurt. Ms. Rose, the teacher, was instructed not to give her good grades and not to be nice to her. Ildiko went to school by herself and was never late. She woke up every day at three o'clock in the morning, so Anna could braid her waist-length hair before going to work in the field. Six months later, Ildiko got her hair cut short. The children were mean to her and the teachers discriminated against her every day. She was never given the grades she deserved. Slowly, Ildiko lost the desire to study. Studying became a chore for her, but she studied hard anyway. She did not want to disappoint her relatives who accepted her into their home.

Communist children had good grades whether they studied or not. They copied each other's papers and loudly helped each other during testing time. The funny thing was that not one teacher ever seemed to notice. One morning, while walking to school, three boys her age attacked Ildiko. She defended herself and they ran away, but were never punished. On several occasions, Ildiko brought bouquets of flowers to her teacher in hopes that the teacher would change her attitude towards her. The teacher never changed; she treated Ildiko the same as before.

On a fall day after school, one of her classmates invited Ildiko to her house. Her parents were in the field, and the children figured they could play. Ildiko was afraid that she was going to get in trouble, but she wanted to make a friend, so she accepted the invitation. After two hours passed, Aunt Anna came and took her home. Ildiko did not get spanked, but her aunt was angry with her. She told her that they were responsible for her safety and she was not to repeat it. It never happened again. There were no friends, only God and her books. Ildiko started to read at a very early age. She read world history, called *The Lexicon, Henry the VIII,* about the regal Bourbon family, the tragic death of Queen Elisabeth and her son Rudolf, *The Tragedy of the Man* by Madack, and all of the Shakespearean dramas. The Madack book presented in Hungarian the story of paradise and the first two human beings, Adam and Eve. That book was very popular at that time and was given to her by the Hungarian language arts teacher. This was the only teacher who was nice to her and gave her the well-deserved grades. She also read *The Last of the Mohicans* and *Uncle Tom's Cabin* with tears in her eyes, realizing once again that people can be really cruel to each other.

In the third grade, there was a school party, similar to Halloween, and the children had a chance to win one of three prizes for the best costume. Anna and her mother made a wonderful costume for Ildiko. She was dressed like a Japanese lady. But she didn't win the first or second prize. She was an "exploiter," so she got third prize. The kind-hearted language arts teacher, knowing that Ildiko loved to read, placed the valuable book as third prize. Ildiko's heart was filled with joy and love for her teacher, Margarett. This teacher, and only this teacher, stood by the truth. There were times when Margarett would argue with the other teachers and even her husband, who was the principal of the school, over Ildiko's discrimination. Margarett became Ildiko's idol. Because of this wonderful teacher, Ildiko decided that one day she would become a schoolteacher. Anna had a big mirror on the living room wall. Many times, Ildiko pretended that the mirror was the class and she was the teacher, just like Margarett.

During that school year, the students who obtained good grades and were well-behaved were distinguished with a red necktie. This necktie was a symbol of the communist flag. The students with these neckties were called "pioneers of the communism." Everyone in the class, besides Ildiko, obtained the red necktie. These students had meetings and different activities to attend. The communist leaders made sure that the children grew up according to the system's beliefs.

CHAPTER 6

"Where Is My Child?"

"She saw a very skinny, tall, gray-haired man."

THE YEARS WENT BY VERY SLOWLY. ANNA'S MOTHER AND ILDIKO spent many late afternoons sitting in the living room in front of the calendar, counting the months, weeks, and days that were left in the year. She was in her 80's, relatively healthy, did some light cooking and washed her own laundry manually.

One spring evening in 1955 when most of the house was sleeping, Anna was still in the kitchen, cleaning up. Ildiko was getting ready for bed when someone quietly knocked on the door. Anna opened the door and rushed into a strange man's arms, whispering "Gabor." Ildiko peeked out of the room to see who it was. She saw a very skinny, tall, gray-haired man. The tall man's first words rang in her ears: "Where is my child?" At that moment, she knew her father had come home. With love in her heart and tears streaming down her face, she ran into her father's outstretched arms. His smiling face was covered in tears as he picked her up to hold her. That night, father and daughter were reunited; they held on to each other all night and did not want to let go. They prayed together, thanking God for

Gabor's freedom. On that night, Ildiko learned how to pray *"Our Father"* and *"I Believe in God."* At dawn, the family found them on their knees praying, this time for Korina's freedom. First it was hard to learn the two prayers, so Gabor was often, patiently helping her out. Before that, she knew only one children's prayer:

" My God, good God,
Slowly I'm closing my eyes,
But yours are always open,
Take care of me while I'm asleep. Amen".

Ildiko was very happy. The warm feeling she had when she saw her father did not leave her heart. She even went to school happy. She did not care about the nastiest teachers, the ones who called her *exploiter.* Everyone noticed the change in her. News travels fast in small towns. Some people secretly rejoiced with Ildiko and her family. The communists hated it. Other people, when approaching Gabor and his daughter on the street, looked around first before they greeted them. Others turned their heads and acted as if no one was there. But it mattered little to Ildiko; her father was home. She couldn't wait to finish her classes. All her free time was spent sitting on his lap. They ate, studied, and prayed together. They did not leave each other, not for a minute. Gabor rested for two weeks, went to see a doctor, and helped Laci out around the house. Finally, he went to see his wife Korina, now as a free man. He promised his daughter that in two months, when she was on summer break, he would return and take her to see her mother. Ildiko was now nine years old and had two more months before third grade was finished. It was extremely hard to let her father go, but in her heart, she knew that he would return for her.

Elementary school picture, Ildiko is the second one in the second row.

CHAPTER 7

The White Handkerchief

"Then Ildiko saw a thin, short, gray-haired women running toward her, waving a white handkerchief."

THOSE TWO MONTHS FELT LIKE TWO YEARS FOR THE LITTLE GIRL. To keep going, she prayed and had many happy thoughts of her parents. In the summer of 1955, Gabor came back for his daughter. He was taking thirteen children to Puiernitza, to see one or both of their parents. Like Korina, their parents were being held in a forced work camp. These children varied in age. All were raised by caring relatives, but unlike Ildiko, they had made this trip before. Gabor had them form a line, and he would count them often to ensure none were left behind.

First, they took the train to Dobrudgea, and then they took a boat from Braila. Finally, after traveling the whole day, they arrived in Puiernitza. There were many people at the shore waiting. The children ran to meet their parents. Gabor was busy getting the bags. Ildiko was standing on the shore, looking at people, while trying to find her mother.

Gabor said to her, "Go to your mother, dear."

His daughter answered sadly, "I don't know which one she is."

Gabor had forgotten for a second that this was her first visit. By that time, only Gabor and his daughter remained on the shore near the boat. Then Ildiko saw a thin, short, gray-haired woman running toward her, waving a white handkerchief. The woman's face was awash with tears, but she was smiling as she hugged her daughter. Mother and daughter were reunited.

Life was hard for the people living in the labor camps. It was hard for Ildiko as well, but she was happy to finally be together with both of her parents. The prickly thorns that grew instead of grass hurt her feet, but she did not seemed bothered by them. Or the so-called outhouse that only consisted of two marks for the feet and a deep hole in between, but not an actual house to cover the area. Or the fact that there were so many people living in one room and all the beds had a really unpleasant smell. The three of them had to sleep in the same twin bed. She did not care about the inedible soup that was their only meal, and the only outside faucet, which she shared with everyone, including the guards. It was very dark at night, since there was no electricity or any oil-burning lamps. Ildiko was very pleased to be with her young but elderly-looking parents.

Each day, Korina brought her a small cup of milk that she hid under her apron. She had to hide it from the guards because it was forbidden, and if caught, she would be punished. Ildiko watched her mother struggle with the thirteen cows every day. The little girl offered her help. After insisting for so long, her mother let her milk the most well-behaved cow Mama, named after Ida Mama. Ildiko milked that cow three times a day for the whole month. Gabor was working there as a builder. They prayed often together. The month passed quickly. Ildiko wanted to stay, but it was too dangerous to attempt it. She had a permit for only one month, and staying would mean the loss of her freedom. Some children did not leave in time and were kept there to work as their parents did. There was no school, and these children did not get the chance to become educated. Korina did not want this for her daughter.

It was time to go. The children kissed their parents, formed a line, and boarded the boat, hoping that they would be able to return next summer. Most were used to it, since they had done this for many years. Ildiko was taking it hard; she had just gotten her mother back and didn't want to leave her. She was hanging on to her mother's neck, screaming, "No, no, no." Everybody was on board and the boat was ready to go. Gabor had to physically separate Ildiko from her mother. The poor child kicked and screamed all the way to the boat. Her father had to unbuckle his leather belt, to strap her to the boat's mast. The boat was finally on its way, yet, despite the engine's noise and the churning water, you could hear the desperate cry of "Mother! Mother!" On the shore, the little, skinny, gray-haired woman's face was wet with tears. She was waving the same white handkerchief and crying out "my child, there goes my child." The guard who escorted her to the shore turned his head away, fighting back tears that this emotional scene evoked.

CHAPTER 8

Reunited

"She no longer was afraid of anyone."

ARRIVING BACK TO BOROSNYO WAS NOT PLEASANT FOR GABOR AND Korina's daughter. To go to the same school and to take the verbal abuse again was bad enough, but the worst was not being able to be with her parents. Gabor had to go back so he could work and earn money to start a new life. He would have worked in the same village, but no one would hire him. He promised to come back again next summer and take her to see her mother. Ildiko was sad. Then she remembered God. From that time on, she turned to God again for help—help to survive without her parents, help to confront all the obstacles in school and in daily life, and help to gain her parents back. The most she prayed for was her mother's freedom. She didn't want to play, or to eat, or even to smile. Ildiko was depressed. All she wanted to do was to pray and read world history books and learned that the truth does not always win. The young girl started to become concerned. What if her father falls from a roof? What if her mother will not be able to keep up with the hard work? Many times during the day, she disappeared from the house and ran to the back yard, hiding between bushes and trees, where she would beg God for help.

In 1956, the Hungarian Revolution broke out. Hungary tried to break away from Russian domination and communism. Even six-year-old children were found fighting against the Russian army. Children and young college students threw themselves in front of the tanks hoping to stop them. They were all crushed to death. Everyone who was able to fight did so, until the Russian tanks made Hungary silent. Many leaders of the revolution were executed. Ildiko remembers listening for hours as the long list of names were read on the radio. She was terrified when she heard a well-known name: Nagy Imre. One of the leaders of the revolution had the same name as her relative. She thought about all the people who had to die by different cruel methods of execution and still could not attain their country's freedom. She prayed for their families, especially for their children. She asked God not to let this massacre be repeated. That night, she could not fall asleep.

Six months passed after the Revolution and she found out how unpredictable and merciful God was. Her mother was released. This happened the same way it had for Gabor. Her release was also due to the many letters, sent to the capital of Romania, Bucharest, from Ajta, demanding her freedom. The people gave evidence and assurance that Korina was innocent. Many of those innocent people remained at the work camps, even twenty years later, and eventually died there. At her release, the Romanian authorities gave her a script, stating that she was a resident of the camp by her own "free" will, and the time she spent at the camp. Ildiko still has this original script.

Although no longer prisoners, Korina and Gabor had a hard time adjusting to society. It was the fifties and times were tough. They had no place to live, but at least they had their freedom and their family was together again. The three of them went to live at Laci's house, who also experienced much hardship and persecution. By that time, all their property and belongings were taken from them. They only had the roof over their heads.

Gabor couldn't get a job in Borosnyo, so he had to work in a different city. He had to run to jump on the train every morning, and jump off it every evening, because the train was a commercial train and did not stop in Borosnyo. One evening, the train conductor noticed Gabor jumping off the train. Every evening after that, the conductor would make an effort to slow the train down when approaching the village. There was no other form of transportation that Gabor could take to work and back. Six months later, with the little money Gabor made, they were able to rent a room. Here Gabor, Korina, Ildiko, and Ida lived a crowded but happy life. There was not enough room for three beds, so at night, the table was turned upside down to serve as a bed for Ildiko. She would sleep on that makeshift bed for years. Finally, she made friends at the school with Kati, Anna, Tercsi, Kato and Adel who came over often to play. One summer day while in the fifth grade Kato invited her to play. They had lots of sheep so the girls started riding them. After riding for hours the poor animals got very tired and they all vent to the barn and laid down. Late evening Kato's parents came home from the field. They were wondering why the sheep are already resting quietly, thank goodness they never found out the truth. In wintertime they went sledging to the"school hill" with many other schoolmates.

This was their new life. It was not easy, but they were together. Ildiko smiled a lot. In the corner, she had a cardboard box with toys made by her mother and Ida. Out of these toys, only one still remains: a doll with the porcelain head. Ildiko's children would treasure that doll for the longest time, as a memory of their mother's childhood. She no longer was afraid of anyone. Her parents were there to back her up. She went to school proud, with a warm feeling in her heart, knowing she had parents at home, just like all the other children. They were there to hug her, kiss her, and reprimand her if it was necessary.

Soon after they moved, Gabor got really sick. He had to take several medications, and Korina had to cook a special diet for him. He eventually got better, but never fully recovered. Most weeks for many years, the train would bring packages of food for the family. There was never a return address. Gabor and Korina never discovered who sent them these packages, but they had an idea. They must have been from the good people of Ajta.

Next to the house where they rented the room was a small garden where Korina planted some vegetables. Most of the time, meals consisted of potatoes and other vegetables, rarely chicken. When packages came with the train, they would have bread, canned food, dried salami, and smoked meat. They felt they were blessed to have such good friends. Sometimes Laci would invite them over for a chicken dinner. Next to Korina's vegetable garden, Ildiko was allowed to grow flowers, which she took good care of.

Very early in the morning, before her father left for work, she could feel a whisper of a kiss on her cheek. Every morning before going to school, her mother hugged and kissed her. After school, she ran into her mother's outstretched arms. This made up for all the unpleasant things that would happen to her at school.

A few years went by. They were able to rent a house with a bedroom, a kitchen, and a porch. Ida and Ildiko slept in the bedroom. Korina and Gabor slept in the kitchen, which was big enough for a stove, a table, four chairs, and a bed. Some nights, when Ildiko was half asleep, she would feel two loving hands covering her with a blanket. Korina would wake up and check on her during cold nights, and if needed, cover the child back up. It was a wonderful feeling to know that in the next room, her beloved parents were sleeping. On the porch, Korina and Ildiko had a lot of flowers. Ida was in her late eighties but would help with the cooking every day. She also made sweaters and fixed any rips and tears in the family's clothing. Korina and Gabor called her Mama, Ildiko named her Mamuka.

Ildiko reunited with her parents.

Sometimes during summer vacations, Ildiko was invited to Gabor's sister Arany's house. She was married to Bela, who was once a judge. Bela lost his job when the communists took over. They had two children, Aranka and Bela Jr. Aranka, as mentioned before, was a schoolteacher who died form a brain tumor. When Bela Jr. grew up to be an adult, he became a lawyer. The communist regime prevented him from practicing his chosen profession. This family was also considered an enemy of communism. Later, when they took everything but the roof over their heads, Bela Jr. worried that he was a burden for his wife, because she was the breadwinner. He committed suicide. He was only fifty-four years old. The pain for Arany and Bela must have been unimaginable, losing both their children. They always seemed very serious and depressed, and treated each other like father and daughter instead of husband and wife. Arany was much younger than her husband. They attended Catholic mass three times a day, along with many other people in their village. The village deserved its name, Saintsoul (Szentlelek).

In the summer of 1958, Ildiko's father took her to visit this couple for two weeks. They were nice to her. Bela Sr. didn't talk much, and Arany made sure the little girl had enough to eat; she thought Ildiko was too thin. It was canning time. In the back yard, they had fruit trees, berry bushes, and a vegetable garden. Arany canned vegetables and fruit so they would have something to eat during the winter months. Ildiko didn't play at all during those two weeks. Since there were no other children to play with, she helped Arany can. She would get up early in the morning and help Arany all day by carrying in wood for the stove, washing dishes, cleaning, and anything else they asked her to do. By evening, she was so tired, she went to bed early. Ildiko did all she could around the house so Arany and Bela would like her. She wanted her parents to be proud of her being well-behaved and helpful.

One night, Ildiko had trouble falling asleep, so she decided to pray, thanking God again for her parents freedom and asking to keep them in good health. The door opened quietly and she heard Arany and Bela enter the room.

Arany said, "Look, dear, how nice and organized she is. This little girl has folded her clothes and put them on the chair. It's amazing how grown up, helpful, and loving she is."

Bela answered, "Yes, dear, like an adult. Poor girl has never really had a childhood."

It felt good for Ildiko to hear these kind words, and she fell asleep with a smile on her face, knowing that Arany and Bela truly cared about her.

At the end of that summer, Ildiko was converted from Reformed religion to the Catholic religion. In Transylvania, girls were baptized after their mother's religion and boys after their father's. Ildiko was baptized Reformed because Korina was Reformed. She had to be converted to the Catholic religion, because Gabor made a promise to God while he was in prison that if he survived, his only child would become Catholic. It was his way of thanking God for their survival. At that time, the Catholic religion was the most powerful religion of all, and most people lived with the idea that it was the most religious way to worship God. The Catholic priest, after a nice service and all kinds of religious examinations, accepted Ildiko as a Catholic. She took this very seriously, because it was her father's wish and now she could practice the most powerful religion. She also loved the ceremony of the Catholic Church.

Shortly after that, Aron Martin Bishop came to Saintsoul, and Ildiko received First Communion from him. This type of thing only happens once in a lifetime. The ceremony was holy and uplifting. The whole town of Saintsoul was there, inside and outside the church. Many children and their families came from other towns of the Saintsoul region. Ildiko didn't know any of them, but felt as they were all close to each other; they had the same God in their hearts. Being a Catholic meant so much to her; she felt like she got closer to God, and this feeling made her very happy. She called the church "God's house." When she entered God's house, she took a deep breath and it felt like there was no more pain, sadness, and discrimination. Happiness, thankfulness, comfort, and warmth moved into her heart. These feelings followed her throughout her life. The time was up; finally she could go home to her parents. The little Hungarian saying fit the event: "Everywhere is good, but the best is at home." Arany and Bela put her on the passenger train, where she met Nagy Imre's son, Elemer, a distant relative by marriage. Korina waited for her in Borosnyo. After hugging each other, they headed for home.

In the fifth grade, a different teacher taught each subject. Ildiko had the pleasure of being in Margarett's class. This was a blessing for her. She also had the misfortune of being in a bloody communist teacher's class. This was the history teacher called Kreiger *elvtars*. *Elvtars* means believing in the same principles. Throughout communism, people were not allowed to address each other as Mister or Missus, only as *elvtars* for the male or *elvtarsno* for the female. He was full of hatred, and punished, and hurt Ildiko's feelings whenever he could. He always asked her the hardest questions and tried to embarrass her in front of the whole class. He purposely spelled out the last three letters of her last name, Szombathy. The *t-h-y* was the sign of nobility for the family. The teacher did not like that. Every time he called on her, he would say: Szomba *t-h-y* Ildiko and he would laugh loudly. The class laughed as well. This is how she was called to the blackboard to recite the lesson. He would interrupt her many times just to confuse her. Kreiger *elvtars* always gave her one or two grades lower then what she deserved. At that time, the grades ranged from one to five (five was the highest grade you could get). Ildiko was very hurt but she never cried. She would not give them the satisfaction of seeing her upset. He also didn't forget to call her "exploiter" every single day. Finally, he died at the age of forty-six from what was at that time an unknown and very painful disease—it could have been cancer.

CHAPTER 9

The Exploiter

"Then she remembered an old Transylvanian saying:
If you don't get educated, you never become a person."

AFTER COMPLETING THE SEVENTH GRADE IN 1959 THEY MOVED TO Kovaszna, where Gabor had his job. This meant that he did not have to jump on and off the moving train anymore. In Kovaszna, they lived in a long barrack-style home near the train station. They had a bedroom, a small kitchen, and a small pantry. Ida and Ildiko had the bedroom; Korina and Gabor had a bed in the kitchen. It felt good to be together, no matter where they lived. That was their home, supported by Gabor's hard work. The neighbors were nice people who treated the Szombathys with respect and dignity. Gabor was an intelligent man. After his graduation from one of Brasso's high schools, he enrolled in Kassa Military Academy as a cadet. So did his brothers Laci and Pista. During the Second World War he fulfilled the ensign rank. Their father Istvan (Steven) Szombathy, born in Kecskemet-Hungary, was an active First Lieutenant in the Royal Hungarian Gendarmie (Csendorseg) in the early 1900s, serving according to their motto: "Faithfully, honorably, valiantly, for my country until death". He married a wealthy widow Janka Bartha in Zagon-Transylvania. During that time the Hungarian officers were not permitted to marry anyone who was "under their rank", meaning that the assets of the bride had to meet a mandated level. Do to his work obligations he was rarely able to go home to Zagon to see his family. At the age of fifty he committed suicide.

Gabor was only twenty years old at the time. He continued school and went home to Zagon often to help his mother with the agriculture. Ildiko was never able to find out why his grandfather died; no one ever talked about that, and she had too much respect for her father to bring up such a painful subject. She questioned herself many times and came up with the same answer, that the following years of World War I and the Trianon Treaty were crucial in Istvan's life. Transylvania was given to Romania and the Hungarian Royal Gendarmie was dismissed. Istvan went home to Zagon just before the border was closed between Hungary and Transylvania. Shortly after that, the manhunt and prosecution of all Hungarian military personnel and anyone associated with, began. Unfortunately, suicide was quite often the resolution to avoid the inevitable, merciless torture exerted on the Hungarian officers in Transylvania. History, like politics, is abstract. It is never reachable, touchable, and there always remain unanswered questions.

The time came for Ildiko to enter the eighth grade. She needed to pass oral and written exams, as well as have a signed document from City Hall stating that her parents were supporters of the Communist Party. When Korina went to enroll her daughter in Kovaszna High School, she was informed that her child did not qualify, because she was a capitalist exploiter.

Korina sadly returned home with the news. She reminded her family not to lose hope, because when a door shuts, a window opens. Brasso High School Number 1 was that window. This school was far away from Ildiko's home in Kovaszna, but it was the only one in Transylvania that did not ask for the document. The admitting exams were extremely hard. There were ten students applying for each opening. The school had only one Hungarian class, with thirty-six children. Almost all of them were coming from the same background. With God's help and her own knowledge, Ildiko passed all exams and was enrolled into the eighth grade. Ildiko was happy to be able to attend Brasso High School, but it would be painful, because her family would be separated once again. Then she remembered an old Transylvanian saying, "If you don't get educated, you never become a person."

On September the fifteenth 1960, Korina and Ildiko traveled to Brasso. Ildiko would be staying in the high school dormitory. These were miserable rooms. One room usually held many children. There were at least two children per bed. The mattresses were stuffed with straw, which made the bed very uncomfortable. Ildiko did not sleep much, so she had plenty of time to think about her parents and the parting from her mother the following day.

Ildiko as a schoolgirl living in the dormitory.

Korina promised to visit once every trimester. They still had uniforms, thick stockings, shoes, school supplies, and the dorm room to pay for; one visit was all they could manage with the money they had earned. Thank goodness makeup and high heels were not permitted. Hair was cut short or worn in braids.

A few months later, they all moved to new dorms. It was far from the high school, but it was a beautiful two-story building with two wings. In the left wing were the boys' rooms, and in the right wing the girls' dormitories. In the middle was the cafeteria or the so-called "lunchroom," which after the meals was transformed into a study hall. At the lower level were the lockers. The front of the building was attached to a huge terrace with stairs on both sides. Even the surrounding area was beautiful. At the back of the building was a wooded part with pretty wildflowers surrounding the edge. The front was also full of beautiful flowers. This house belonged to a family before the *naturalization,* and that family sure knew how to pick a gorgeous place to build a home. The bedrooms had big windows and balconies. There were four to six beds in one big bedroom, to accommodate the new scholars. Throughout the wintertime, in the snow and in the spring and fall rain, every morning they would walk in a straight line two by two toward the school. The school did not have money for bus transportation. The Romanian language arts educator watched over them and escorted them to the school and back. Ildiko was unhappy the first year until her summer vacation, when she was able to return home. While spending the summer in Kovaszna, she met a girl her age and they became friends. Her new friend, Ildiko Balint taught her a couple of funny songs. When Ildiko sang them in school, she became more and more popular. Every evening, someone would ask her to sing. "The Jampy Child" was the one song the children requested most. To this day, she still remembers this song.

A Jampi Gyerek

I

Elment a jampi gyerek csorogni
Mindenki rajta kezdett rohogni
Ugy allt a nadrag szara mint a kalyhacso
Nyakaban logott a ket jampi no

II

Kriptaban tancolnak a halottak
Labszaron szakszizik az egyik tag
Koponyan dobol a csontvaz
A masik keveri a rumbat, a rumbat, a rumbat

English translation: The Jampi Child

I

The Jampi child went to rock
Everybody started to laugh
His pants looked like stovepipes
On his neck two Jampi girls were hanging

II

All the dead are dancing in their grave
One plays the saxophone on a leg bone
The skeleton drums on the skull
The others are dancing the rumba

From that point on, all the students called her *"Jampi Gyerek."* The seniors made her feel special; there were many nights she was invited to their dorm to sing. During that time, a Romanian senior girl named Valentina mothered her. She would comb Ildiko's hair, hug her, and give her candy. Life seemed better. This attention helped to lessen the uncertainty of starting a new life, and helped relieve some of the longing for her parents.

One night, after singing and dancing, Ildiko heard clapping coming from the direction of the windows. Looking out, she saw that a group of boys from her class were enjoying the song. Some evenings after *silencium,* the studying hour, the educator let the students play in the dorms' yard. The new dance in style was a combination of polka with running back and forth and switching partners. Everybody loved it because it was one of the very few times the girls and the boys could interact. On some Sundays, if students had good grades and behaved well during the week, the educator let them leave the dorms between 4 pm and 8 pm. It was movie time. The boys with the boys and the girls also with only girls went to see a movie. At that time, not many students dated before graduating high school.

When Ildiko was in the tenth grade, Ida Mama fell and broke both hips. Shortly after the fall, at the age of ninety-two, Ida Mama passed away. Ildiko, losing the dearest and most loving grandmother figure, was heartbroken.

During the tenth grade summer vacation, her friend—the one who taught her the *Jampi Gyerek* song—invited Ildiko to a *"hazi-buli,"* which means "little afternoon snack and dance party." At this party, she danced for the first time with a boy she liked. A few days later, that boy invited her to the movies. They got along well had a good time together. Not too long after that, the boy and his family moved away to a different city. Ildiko only saw him once again briefly, nine years later.

September the fifteenth 1963 arrived, and it was time to go back to school to start the eleventh grade. Mom thought it would be nice for her senior daughter to have a permanent put in her hair. What Korina didn't know was that perms were against school policy. As punishment for breaking policy, the principal took two points away from Ildiko's "good behavior" grade. The other students laughed at her and teased her by saying, "You look like an Easter lamb!" This event harmed her popularity with the other students.

In Romania during the 1960's, high school ended after the completion of eleventh grade. For most people graduating and earning a high school diploma was a big event. As the end of the last semester neared, the seniors were busy preparing for their written and oral exams. These exams would cover eight subjects. To lessen the pressure, on Saturdays the dorm coordinator would let them dance in the corner of the dining room while listening to a phonograph. Ildiko enjoyed the dancing. Not many students knew how to dance, and the ones who did only knew one dance—the tango. This was some kind of European tango, two steps forward and one back. So whoever wanted to learn this dance, the educator was willing to teach them the steps. Ildiko knew this dance from her girlfriend in Kovaszna. This dancing was the only fun they had as a class before graduating.

Ildiko had a classmate who liked to dance with her. She danced with him on occasion, but not as many times as he wanted. On one occurrence, he was mad and called her "Miss Too-good." That boy was from Ajta, the same place where Ildiko's parents were *naturalized,* and he knew of her family. Others picked up on it too, and soon several boys called her "Miss." She felt hurt by the boys' teasing. If she could have seen into the future and known that one day her daughter would be called Miss, to show honor, she probably would have been pleased rather than hurt.

A few weeks before final exams, Ildiko was diagnosed with the mumps. Since the mumps is transmittable, she had to be isolated for six weeks. To keep her away from the rest of the student body, she was placed in the attic, which felt like a prison. The dietitian would bring up her meals and leave them on the top step. Few visitors came to see her, and when they did, all conversation had to be through a closed door. With so few interruptions, she had plenty of time to study, pray, and think. When the six lonely weeks were over, she had missed the exams and would have to wait to take them in the summer.

Summer finally arrived, and Ildiko went home to Kovaszna. She visited Laci and his family in Borosnyo, and then went to see her aunt and grandparents in Besenyo. It was wonderful to be in Besenyo again after so many years. She climbed her trees and went into the forest to pick mushrooms and strawberries. It seemed the only change in the hidden village was that the people had gotten older. She enjoyed a restful week at Grandma's house. They ate lots of fresh vegetables, but the best was still the chicken paprikas that Grandma made.

A few days passed and Grandma fell and hit her head. Blood was running from the wound. Because there was not a doctor in the hidden village, Ildiko ran to the neighbor and asked him for help. The neighbor agreed to take them to the village of Maksa, which was two miles away. The only type of transportation the neighbor had was a buggy with two skinny horses. Grandma and Ildiko climbed into the buggy. Grandma laid her head in Ildiko's lap because the trip would take a couple of hours on the dirt road. Grandma bled through everything. Ildiko prayed that Grandma would still be alive when they arrived to the doctor, but then she remembered that Grandma served in World War I as a nurse. She was a tough woman. When they reached the doctor's office, they realized that he was alone, so Ildiko was needed to assist him. Grandma's wound had to be stitched up. Grandma made it through the procedure fine, but Ildiko fainted.

On the way back to Besenyo, Ildiko had plenty of time to think about her grandmother and grandfather's relationship. Grandma Korina lived in the village with her children, while Grandpa Zoltan lived in a wooden cottage in the middle of one of his forests. He lived with Ilus, who once was Grandma's maid. I guess in many of the wealthier families, it was common for the gentleman of the house—mostly the ones who were not married—to spend their lives with one of the housemaids. Therefore, when the family got together, particularly during the holidays, Grandpa Zoltan came down from the forest and stayed at the house, but had his own room. When he became very old, he moved back to the village, since Ilus did not want to take care of him. He was a very tall man with a long mustache. At nighttime, he wore a mustache holder and a nightcap.

Maybe Grandma Korina—who was beautiful and young—married Grandpa because her parents expected her to. This way, they would unite the wealth of the two families. In Transylvania, this was a very common way of uniting two noble families. But these marriages lacked love. Ildiko's parents were lucky. Both were young and, in truth, nice looking, and they fell in love with each other at first sight. That was one of the very rare successful arranged marriages.

Not one person volunteered to tell Ildiko about her grandparents strange living arrangement. Ildiko thought it would be discourteous and uncomfortable to ask about it. One of the few things she heard was that before Grandma Korina was married she was often invited to Vienna to the ball of Majesty Franz Joseph, and that the Austrian royals enjoyed her company. Ildiko saw several pictures of them.

CHAPTER 10

The Warm Wind-like Touch

"On August 12, 1967 the most darling, sweet and handsome baby boy was born, named Bela Jr."

SOON, SUMMER VACATION WAS OVER AND IT WAS TIME FOR ILDIKO to pack and go home to Kovaszna. Before she knew it, she was on her way to Vasarhely to take her entrance exams for college. Her dream was to become a schoolteacher. History was her favorite subject, but she objected teaching a history that was twisted to fit the Communist point of view. The subjects that she decided to teach were Hungarian-Romanian languages. The entrance exam was extremely hard; there were fifteen students for every one placement. Luck was with her; no one asked to see the document from City Hall. She passed the exams with God's help, and in fall of 1964 entered college.

At the end of the first year, she met her first love Bela. He studied at the same college. They dated and were married in 1965, against the wishes of Ildiko's parents.

Ildiko started teaching in a Romanian village called Moisa, close to Vasarhely, where she continued her education. On August 12, 1967 the most darling, sweet and handsome baby boy was born, named Bela Jr.

Unfortunately, the marriage did not work, and two years after the birth of Bela Jr.,mother and son moved back to Kovaszna to stay with Ildiko's parents. Bela Jr. was everything to Ildiko: her happiness and her life. He also helped fulfill the life of his grandparents. He replaced the loss of nurturing their daughter at that age. Soon he went to kindergarten and made lots of friends. He also took dance lessons and performed Hungarian popular dances. Everybody loved him. Ildiko hoped that all the love he received from his family made up for the loss of his father. To this day, when Ildiko looks at her son, she is reminded of her father, Gabor. Bela Jr. has inherited Gabor's honesty, kindness, and generosity. It still hurts to think that Bela Jr. had to grow up without his biological father; only God knows if it was better that way.

One day, Korina's friend Margit came from Canada to visit. They emigrated during the Second World War. At that time, they asked Korina and Gabor to go with them, but like good patriots, they didn't go. "Dear parents, how wrong were you!" Their country put its good patriots through hell. Margit, her husband and sons established a good life in Canada. She talked about freedom of religion, speech, and about the free world leader, the United States of America.

All through the year, Ildiko was teaching in another city, traveling by train or bus every day. One day, she was watching the students during an outside ten minutes school recess when something made her look up. The sky was the most beautiful blue and not one cloud could be seen. The day was still, and she thought, *spring is here.* Suddenly Ildiko remembered the conversation with Margit, sighed and said, "Oh, God, I wish I could go to America and visit." She didn't dare say the wish that was really in her heart: to leave her country. She stood very still looking up, when she felt a warm wind-like touch on her face. It was very mysterious, uplifting and promising. Then she heard the school bells ring; recess was over. It was time to head back indoors for classes. She smiled; how she loved to teach.

It has to be mentioned here that under the domination of President Ceausescu and his wife Elena, no one could visit the "West" unless they had strong connections with the Communist leaders. Ildiko and her family were labeled; she couldn't even dream of visiting the United States. The *Securitate* (secret police) and police would never honor her application for a Romanian passport.

Ildiko as a schoolteacher in the small village.

CHAPTER 11

Life's Struggles

"After four years of marriage, on August 1975, Ildiko gave birth to a beautiful baby girl, Melinda, everyone adored her."

AFTER FOUR YEARS OF HARD WORK, ILDIKO SPENT HER WELL-DESERVED vacation in Sovata, a small city in Transylvania known for its healing waters and resorts. Here she met Elemer, a childhood friend, who was also spending his vacation at Sovata. They had not seen each other in fifteen years.

Elemer was a flutist in the symphony orchestra in Szatmar, a city in the northwest corner of Transylvania near the Hungarian border. He was vacationing with some of his colleagues and their families from Szatmar. Elemer had only five days left of his vacation. They hardly recognized each other, but soon realized that they had more than a feeling of friendship for each other. Four days later, Elemer called the director of the symphony orchestra and requested five more days off, to get married.

What did this marriage mean for Ildiko? She had to leave home, quit work—a job she loved—but more importantly, she had to leave her beloved son. At this time, Elemer had only one room to live in. Everyone in the orchestra, including the director, was very nice to her. She was able to find a teaching position in a nearby village to Szatmar. Ildiko had to travel by bus every day. The day came when gasoline was restricted and the buses were no longer running. The teachers and nurses had to find other modes of transportation. There was not much choice but to find a ride by horse and buggy to get to their jobs. When winter came, the horse-and-buggy rides were no longer available. Because of this, she was out of a job. After that, she was a little unhappy at the start of every new school year.

Elemer's director hired her as the music librarian, and later she worked as the Symphony's secretary. Because she heard the classical music so much, she grew fond of it. Ildiko and Elemer saved their money for many years to buy a car. By the time they were able to afford it, the gasoline was being rationed again. The gas coupon was good for one week during every month.

Bela Jr. celebrated his sixth birthday in 1973 and came to Szatmar to start school. It was hard to leave his grandparents and come to a strange city to live with a father he didn't know. He had no friends, no neighbors to play with, just his mother who loved him dearly. When Bela Jr. saw his mother, his whole face lit up with joy.

Soon it was time for him to start school. He made friends with classmates and neighbors quickly. He was the teacher's favorite; many times she took him home with her after school. Food, just like gasoline, was also rationed. There was never enough to eat. The teacher would cook for him; she loved to see him eat. I'm sure Bela Jr. liked her food more than her teaching. He didn't have a problem adapting to this new life.

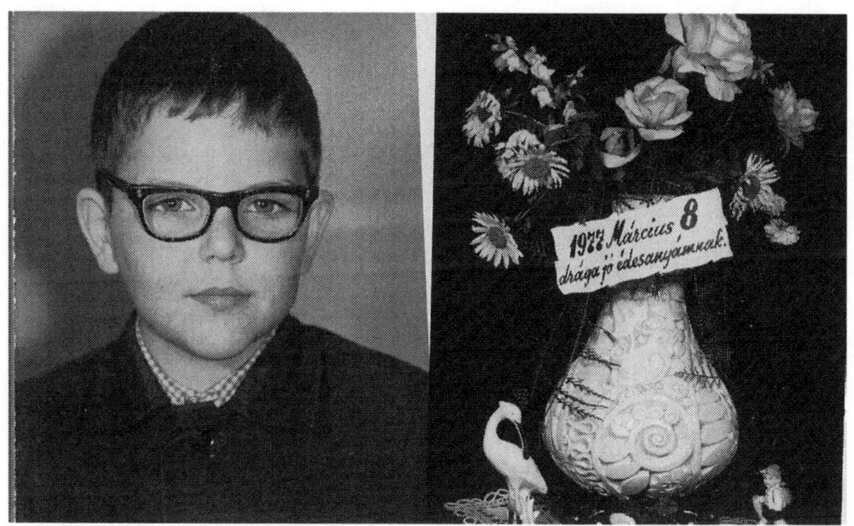

Mother's Day card from Bela Jr.

After four years of marriage, on August third 1975, Ildiko gave birth to a beautiful baby girl, Melinda, everyone adored her. Ildiko's second pregnancy was also very hard. She spent most of the time in the hospital receiving tube feeding, because she was unable to keep anything down. Maybe this is the reason that she was and still is an overprotective parent.

At Szatmar's birthing center, Ildiko had to wait in line to give birth; she was the thirteenth pregnant patient that night. There were not enough doctors or nurses. When it was finally her turn, the doctor did not have time to make an incision, and she was torn during the birthing process. After the baby arrived, the nurse pushed Ildiko's stretcher into the hallway while she attended to the other patients in line. She waited in pain for more than two hours. Finally the nurse started stitching her up without giving her any anesthetic. Ildiko did not make any noise. The nurse told her to just go ahead and scream; she understood that it was very painful. But Ildiko did not have that much strength in her. In her mind, she was thinking of the baby, hoping she was healthy and safe. The doctor was very busy, but had to comment on how beautiful and round Melinda's head was.

Two weeks after Melinda was born, Ildiko got sick with the mumps for the second time. She had to be separated from everyone. Korina came to help with the new baby girl. A few times every day, Elemer or Korina would bring the baby to the door so Ildiko could see her. It made her more miserable, because she could not kiss or hold her baby. There was no baby formula available, so Ildiko had to pump milk six times a day for the baby. Korina would boil it to make sure it would not carry any bacteria to the newborn.

Life became harder and harder in Romania under the Ceausescu regime. Minorities were not treated equally. The economy was at ground level; there was hardly any food. Citizens stood in line in front of the stores, no matter what the season was. Bitter cold winter or hot summer, days and sometimes nights before the stores even opened for business. Family members took turns standing in line, especially in the wintertime. There was a lot of pushing and arguments heard in these food lines, mostly out of desperation and frustration because of the horrible situation. Everyone had at least one child at home to feed. Some women tried to put pillows under their coats to look as if they were pregnant, hoping to get ahead in the line. But most people stood in line and prayed that the stores didn't run out of food before they got to the counter.

The majority of this burden fell on Korina, since she did all the cooking in the home. For example: a half-liter of oil per family for one month. If they were lucky, they were able to get meat once a week. Families with children three years and under could get a liter of milk every other day. The milk was so thin that after you emptied the glass, it was clean. People who came from Hungary brought some food across the border. If you were lucky enough, you could find out where it was and you purchased it for three times the amount of what it was worth. In other words, it was a major challenge just to get enough food for your family to survive.

Water was also a big problem. There was a schedule that was not always followed. They only had warm water a couple of times a week; cold water was in the morning between 6:00 and 8:00, and then again in the evening between 5:00 and 7:00. Electricity was interrupted throughout the day, with steady current between 7:00 pm and 9:00 pm. Soon the stores ran out of candles. There was almost no heat; it was controlled by the city. They tried to keep the baby's room warm by using the stove from the kitchen. Melinda still remembers her sheets tucked in so tightly that she couldn't uncover herself. The poor little girl had strep throat almost every month; she had to get lots of penicillin injections. She received so many that she started to hide under the bed every time she saw the nurse. Once she put a little box under the rug in hopes that the nurse would trip and fall. These were the few times that Melinda misbehaved in her childhood. Most of the time she was quiet and serious.

Soon Korina had to go home, and Melinda had to go to daycare. Ildiko's workday started at 7:00 am and Elemer's at 9:00 am. So Elemer would take her to daycare every morning, five days a week. In the wintertime, he would wrap her in such a big blanket that the end would drag in the snow. Daycare in Romania was not like the American daycare. Food was of poor quality; most of the time there was no toilet paper. Elemer found out later from a friend's daughter who worked there that the children were all being wiped with the same cloth because nothing else was available. They were all using the same silverware and the same pacifier without washing it in between children.

Easter 1975, Bela Jr. attended second grade. Knowing how much he liked sweets, Korina mailed the family a big box of goodies. There was one specific kind of cake called *jerbo pite,* which was Bela Jr.'s favorite. The cake had many thin layers with fruit jelly in between and chocolate frosting on top. Korina cut up the cake to fit in the box with the other cookies and put a thin sheet of wax paper between the slices. The chocolate frosting melted and hid some of the wax paper. Bela Jr., not knowing this, began eating the slice of cake with such a good appetite, not noticing that the paper was going down as well. When the parents noticed, they pulled it out of his mouth and they all had a good laugh. This was one of their favorite memories during the hard times.

In the meantime, Melinda was struggling with tonsillitis. After many battles and a lot of antibiotics, the doctor decided to take out her tonsils at the young age of three. At the time, the doctors and equipment were not very advanced, Ildiko and Elemer were very concerned about the surgery. They were not the only ones. The surgery went well. Melinda was still sleeping from the medication when a little boy sneaked into the hospital to check on his sister. There were no visitors allowed in the unit besides the parents. Bela Jr. went into the room where all the other children were recovering, kissed his sister on the cheeks, and ran back out to play. He loved and cherished his sister. Ildiko had a warm feeling inside her, knowing that her children were so close. She knew that her children's relationship would just grow stronger as time passed, and they will support each other when her time will come.

Time passed, and their difficult life continued just as it did before. Melinda started the first grade in 1981. Since gymnastics was a major sport in all the Eastern Block countries, her parents enrolled her in gymnastics school, which was on the other side of the city. If you advanced to the national level in a sport like gymnastics or soccer, you received special privileges. These included being allowed to leave the country for tournaments, privileges regarding food and clothing, and altogether a better life. Here you had to pass a physical test to be able to attend the school. Every school day, you trained in gymnastics. Melinda liked gymnastics a lot. She also had some very good friends in her class. Again, there was not enough gas to drive to school every day. Many times, Melinda walked home from school carrying her heavy red leather backpack full of books. When she got home, her back was aching. She kept her mind on her studies and there were never any complaints about her at school. At the end of each school year, she obtained an honor roll certificate that she was proud of. But still her favorite thing to do was to play outside with her best friend Andrea.

Mother's Day card from Melinda.

CHAPTER 12

Expelled

"Once there, he was ordered to end Ildiko's work contract immediately."

It was the summer of 1984. The Szatmar Symphony Orchestra organized a classical music tour to Italy, as they had done every summer for the past eight years. The musicians performed classical music, pop music, ballet music, and overtures to operas. The symphony's director along with the president of the Communist Party and the maintenance man, escorted them everywhere in order to insure that all members of the orchestra return to Romania. They had their eyes and ears open day and night. The musicians performed in many cities and in many churches, since the Italian churches are famous for their wonderful acoustics. The orchestra performed well and the audience was enthusiastic.

Finally, the three weeks were up and the last concert was being played. This was the time when the musicians who did not want to return to Romania had a very difficult decision to make. If they were caught, they would be dragged back to Romania and prosecuted harshly or probably killed as an example of a bad communist citizen.

If they were to sneak out of the dorm room successfully, where would they go without knowing the language? Would anyone help them? Or would they hand them over to the Romanian authorities? What about the family members who were still at home? How would they be treated?

That year, Elemer had the chance to go with the orchestra to Italy as a flutist, and made a wise decision not to return to Romania. Perhaps this decision was very difficult, but it had to be done. He spent six months in the biggest Italian refugee camp, called "Latina." Here he took any job he could find. He picked tomatoes in the heat during the day and watched the gates of the camp at night. He also worked for a company moving pianos into houses. Elemer was not used to the hard physical labor, but he knew he had no other choice if he wanted to see his wife and children again. While living in the camp, Elemer applied for political asylum to the United States. His request was granted in March of 1985, sponsored by the Lutheran Immigration. They helped him find a job and a place to live. The Lutheran Church made sure his family would come as soon as possible. Fortunately, there was an international law referring to the unification of families.

The United States Immigration office is always overwhelmed, because thousands of people are wishing to enter the country every day, and also thousands of refugees are begging to stay. As busy as they were, it took only twenty months for Elemer to have his family's visa handed to him.

Back in Romania, due to the fact that Elemer did not return home, his family was expelled from society. Some of their so-called friends would turn their heads when they saw them coming. Others would cross and walk on the other side of the street to avoid conversation. Some of these people were jealous that the family had their greatest wish granted. But most of these people were afraid the *Securitate*—the secret service—would see them talking with the people going to the West. If they were caught, it could cost them their jobs or worse. Because of Ildiko's childhood, she did not find it to difficult to survive without socializing with other people. But this time, it was different; she had hopes that it would end soon and they would be able to live a fair, free life with no boundaries.

As soon as the musicians came back from Italy, the director of the Symphony Orchestra was summoned to the main office of the Communist Party. Once there, he was ordered to end Ildiko's work contract immediately. When he returned to his office, he explained to her what happened and told her she no longer had a job. Deep down, he knew that this order was unfair.

Ildiko traveled to Bucharest, the capital of Romania, to the Romanian Embassy numerous times, in order to get the Romanian Embassy's permission to leave the country. After Elemer applied for political asylum, she was ordered to City Hall. The officials there informed her that Elemer's half of their house now belonged to the state, and that when she obtained her visa to "the West" (the United States), the other half would have to be sold to the state.

The family had little money; Ildiko had to sell the car and most of their furniture to make ends meet. The parents on both sides shared food with the family. Also, a few good friends including Emma made sure that the family did not go hungry while living in Szatmar. She was a nurse in Vetes, a nearby village, and knew some of the farmers who would sell her pork, chicken, eggs, milk, and cheese. She was one of the few good friends who would secretly help the family, even though they had little themselves. They will always be remembered with much gratitude.

In the summer of 1985, a very significant event took place: Korina and Gabor's fiftieth wedding anniversary. Ildiko wanted to do something very special for her loving parents. Knowing that Gabor and Korina were religious, she thought it would be a great gift to have a service in their honor at the biggest Hungarian Catholic church in Szatmar. They were invited to Szatmar, and the following day, they all went to the church. The church was decorated with beautiful flowers. Peace, silence, and harmony filled the air. The father had a touching speech about the fifty years the couple spent married. The organist played beautiful, well-known hymns. And the icing on the cake was that Bela Jr. served as the altar boy, which made his grandparents very proud. The ceremony was inspiring and holy; the couple had tears in their eyes. There was a feeling of closeness, love, appreciation, and thankfulness for being together.

CHAPTER 13

Unpredictable Accidents

"As he laid on the ground, she made sure her son was alive and then took off after the man."

IT WAS THE SPRING OF 1986. BELA JR. WAS GETTING READY TO GRADUATE high school, and Melinda was in the fourth grade at the gymnastics school. Ildiko's thoughts were always with her children. The only time she was not with them was during school hours. She was afraid for their lives. The children were not allowed out after dark. The power was not turned on until 7:00 pm. They would sit in the dark and cover up with blankets to keep warm. Ildiko would entertain them with stories about their family and friends. During these cold, dark hours, they learned to sing popular Hungarian folk songs. There was talk of families who chose to leave the country having accidents: car, motorcycle, falling from the third floor at work. People called these "unpredictable accidents."

Ildiko had to travel to the Romanian Embassy many times to plead for their visa. The authorities of the Communist Party and police delayed it as much as possible. In Szatmar every Monday, they would find her knocking on the police bureau's door, asking for a hearing in this matter. The police and the secret service were the main dictators, as they were employed everywhere. It must have been hard to follow all the people who wanted to leave the country, report on them, and make their lives miserable and full of fear.

Most of the Communist and police officials would attend the symphony, not because they enjoyed the music or had been musically inclined, but because it was elegant and stylish, and most educated people attended weekly. The director of the orchestra would provide them with coffee and sweets—desserts that ordinary citizens could not even dream of touching. Ildiko would have to serve them. The officials and their bodyguards never had to pay for admission, and they had the best seats in the house. Because they knew Ildiko from the concerts, they let her family go to the United States a lot faster than others. If she had bribed them, they would have agreed to let her go even sooner.

Because Bela Jr. and Melinda were still in school, they could not leave Szatmar until the summer vacation began. Bela Jr. loved to spend time with his grandparents in Kovaszna, helping them out around the house. He had many great friends there. He spent every summer vacation with them, and visited his biological father and family. Melinda liked spending time there also. She would help Gabor water the plants, went with him on his daily walks and enjoyed talking with him about old times. Korina cooked delicious Hungarian dishes for her because she found her to be too thin. Korina was younger and healthier than Gabor. She did all the housework, shopping, and cooking. She cooked three times a day. For Gabor she made foods recommended by the doctor. He had never really gotten well; he still had stomach problems and many times he passed blood. His legs hurt him severely from the arthritis mostly at nighttime. He tried to be very quiet, but his daughter could hear him in the next room, the deep painful struggle every night. The pain medication did not help anymore. Ildiko took him for walks in the afternoon so he could feel better physically and emotionally, and to spend quality time with her father. Gabor was always a very thoughtful man. After the walks, he would kiss her cheeks and say, "Thank you, my dear daughter."

Ildiko could not help but wonder: Why do people do terrible things to each other? Who has the right to make one's life miserable? Why did those awful things happen to Gabor and his family? How can the people who inflicted so much pain on others still be free to live their lives unaffected? Do we always have to be alert to find out others' intentions, whether they are good or not? Why do we have to be suspicious of people we do not know, in order not to have unpleasant surprises and not to get hurt by their actions or behaviors? Is the drive for money taking over people's lives, and there is no more room for nice thoughts, actions, comfort, generosity, or love toward each other as God taught us? All these questions seem simple but get very complicated and difficult to experience in real life.

Money was very low and Bela Jr., being the man of the house, started to work for a construction company. The work was hard and the wages were poor, but it brought money into the house. A few months later, he had to stop working. Late one afternoon, Bela Jr. was outside with his friends when a man suddenly appeared and started to beat him with a bat. Ildiko, who had been watching the kids from the kitchen window, saw what happened and raced down the stairs. As he laid on the ground, she made sure her son was alive and then took off after the man. The man had gone a distance, but could still be seen. She ran as fast as she could but was unable to catch him. Ildiko will never forget what he looked like. He was short but muscular, and was wearing a cream-colored coat and dark blue pants. He looked like the maintenance man from the orchestra; even the color of his hair was the same. The secret service had placed this man in the Philharmonic to keep an eye on everyone and to report what he had seen.

Finally, summer vacation started. Bela Jr. and Melinda finished school and they moved to a safer place. The move took them back to Ildiko's parents' home in Kovaszna. Before they left, a City Hall representative took the house keys and made Ildiko sign a document that stated they would not move back there. They were also followed in Kovaszna, but it was less threatening with her parents there. A few times, they went to visit Elemer's parents and spent time with them. Elemer's parents, Imre and Iren, had a farm near Malnas, a pretty little village at the pillar of the Harghita mountain. The Harghita mountain is built of crystalline rocks and reaches a peak of 7,556 feet. The time spent there was quiet, peaceful without disturbances.

It felt tremendous to be free of stress and fear, to sleep less vigilantly, to wake up to the churning of the water at the back of the house, and to breathe in the fresh air brought by the winds from the closest forests of the Carpathian Mountains. This peaceful scenario suddenly ended after returning to Kovaszna.

The next day, in the summer of 1986, a major nuclear plant exploded in Cernobil - Russia. From Kovaszna to Cernobil over the Carpathian Mountains the distance is like from Detroit to Chicago. The public was never notified. For two weeks after the explosion, the sky was cloudy and it was drizzling day and night. Two weeks later, Hungary conducted a test and concluded that the radiation was eight to ten times higher than it should have been. The Romanian authorities began to distribute expired iodine tablets to keep the people calm. Panic was setting in. There was nowhere to hide. The air was contaminated and it had been for weeks. The initial damage was done without any warnings. Trapped, people went on with their everyday activities as much as possible. The radiation was so strong that on the East Coast of the United States, it was noticeable. Thousands if not millions of people were affected by this accident. Many died, some developed life-threatening illnesses; pregnant women during that period gave birth to deformed babies. It was a very unfortunate situation. American doctors believe that the radiation caused hyperthyroidism in Ildiko. Some of Melinda's lymph nodes grew big, and at age twenty-one, Bela Jr. was diagnosed with cancer.

Ildiko with Bela Jr. and Melinda, last picture in Transylvania.

CHAPTER 14

Let Freedom Ring

"For the first time in their lives, they experienced freedom."

FINALLY, IN DECEMBER OF 1986, ELEMER WAS ABLE TO SEND THE United States welcome visa to his family dated for December the 10th. Ildiko knew that her most desired dream was soon to become true. A new, unknown, but very pleasant feeling took over the fear, stress, and frustration: happiness, hope for a free and safe life, knowing that no one will ever harm her or her children. It will be done and over with the Communist-created persecutions, and their struggles were about to end forever.

It was time to say goodbye to parents and other relatives such as Gabi, Laci, Pistu, and Eva, and discreetly to the few remaining friends they had. Bela Jr. and Melinda said so long to their friends in Kovaszna and Szatmar. Ildiko has always wondered about her children's feelings, leaving behind their relatives and friends. She never asked them, but looking into their eyes, she saw sadness for leaving their grandparents but also happiness and trust for the future and lots of excitement.

Each person was allowed to take on the airplane a twenty-kilogram suitcase and a carry-on bag. They packed only the most sentimental objects, some Hungarian authentic embroidery, a few pictures of their family and friends.

Ildiko hugged and kissed her father Gabor for the last time; they all realized they would not see him again. Ildiko experienced the pain she felt long ago when she had to leave her mother in Puiernita, Dobrogea just before summer vacation ended. Her heart was aching and her mind said, *"Father, Father, my dear good father, I have to leave you. I don't want to let you down. I know I'll never see you during this lifetime, only up in heaven. My dear father, I am not leaving you for myself, but my children are innocent; they need a fair life. Goodbye, my dear father."* Although these words never left her lips, her father felt them and could see them in her eyes.

Two friends were holding Gabor's arms at the train station; he didn't cry, just hugged his daughter and whispered into her ear, "Go, my child, and God bless you." He looked very calm. He stood there, tall and thin like a tree after a storm with ripped and broken branches, quietly ready to collapse. At that time, he was almost eighty years old and very ill.

Korina was only seventy-two years old and in fairly good health. Her tears were dripping on her shirt, but under the tears, Ildiko could see a little smile. She knew it would be a long time before she would see her daughter and grandchildren, but was happy because they were on their way to the light of freedom. As the train pulled away from the station, the three of them could not turn away from the elderly couple's slowly disappearing silhouette.

From Bucharest, the capital of Romania, they departed for Athens, Greece. The small Romanian plane was very noisy and wavering. When they landed in Greece, it was warm. For the first time in their lives, they experienced freedom. For Ildiko, freedom meant self-esteem, happiness, no boundaries, and safety. There was an unusual fresh, inspiring fragrance in the air and sunshine in the heart. The family spent one day and one night in Greece. During the day, they walked around the ocean shore without any money. Melinda stopped in front of a little store with all kinds of sweets. She wanted something. Ildiko offered her perfume in exchange for sweets. The salesman declined, but gave Melinda a little bit of chocolate anyway. The chocolate tasted good; it was the best piece of chocolate she'd ever had. In the meantime, Bela Jr. was sunbathing on the hotel's balcony.

The next day, they boarded a Greek airplane named *Olympic* and flew from Greece to New York City. This was a beautiful, elegant plane; it held close to three hundred happy passengers. The food and drinks were delicious and free. Bela Jr. and Melinda were delighted. In twelve hours, they were approaching New York City. The Statue of Liberty stood proud and tall, shining over the ocean. She was even more beautiful at night with all the lights on the ground. It was breathtaking to see the massive Twin Towers glowing prominently on the island of Manhattan. The view was unforgettable. The family was exhausted but overjoyed; in their minds, they saw only one word, "FREEDOM." Seeing that they were so excited, people tried to talk to them. The family just smiled; they didn't understand one word but knew they were being welcomed.

December 12, 1986 at 5:00 pm, they arrived in New York at the JFK Airport, which looked like a big city. A Lutheran Immigration representative handed them the "Welcome to America" card. Ildiko was crying of happiness. In the following two hours waiting to depart, she felt sorry for her parents, but she also felt strong enough to start a new free life. She knew it would be a long time until they could show true happiness, and then they would be freed of the haunting pressure of the past. The past stays with a person; they carry it into the present willingly or unwillingly. It takes work to be unchained of unpleasant events. For now, it was the freedom they were longing for.

That night at 9:00 pm, they arrived to Metropolitan Detroit, their final destination. This was even more special because it was Christmastime and the city was festively decorated. The Communist system does not recognize God, and the citizens are not allowed to celebrate Christmas. However, Ildiko, Bela Jr., and Melinda were finally here in America—*from the darkness of Communism to the light of Freedom.*

Ildiko looked up at the sky and saw the moon and millions of stars shining down onto the Earth. Her heart was overflowing with happiness and thankfulness. Suddenly she felt a little warm wind-like touch caress her face, just like she had twenty years ago in the schoolyard when she made her wish.

God granted her wish to live the rest of her life in freedom and peace in the strongest and most respected leader of the free world, the United States of America.

THANK YOU

TESTIMONY

Korina Szombathy

My name is Korina Szombathy, I am a 74 years old woman from Transylvania, Romania (a region originally and rightfully a part of Hungary) and my mother tongue is Hungarian. I set down here briefly the details of the persecution I endured at the hands of the Communist order.

At the end of World War II in Eastern and Central Europe in 1945, the Russians won. That was the onset of communism in this region, a communism that denies the existence of God, and persecutes anyone who does not uphold those views. People who supported communism eagerly awaited the development of the new order since the King had been dethroned. But we who were opposed to it trembled and feared what was to come. We lived in the heart of the residential area in Ajta. We owned the land and lived in the home of our ancestors: men who earned every bit of the land beneath their feet. By 1947 the Communist Party was well established and their slogan, one of many, frequently heard was "Down with the rotten capitalists".

It was in 1949 late at night, when they rattled our windows and demanded that we immediately open up. When my husband, Gabor Szombathy, opened the door armed communists and party leaders rushed into our home. At gun point they gave us ten minutes to dress and board one of the waiting freight trucks which were already filled with many people from the surrounding regions. Our little girl, Ildiko, was only two and a half years old at the time. We dressed quickly. We were also required to turn all our money over. Time was up. They surrounded us, then like criminals shackled my husband and forced us on one of the trucks.

We did not know our destination. I thought we wouldn't stop until we reached Siberia, Russia. The guards and the night made it impossible to look out and see our surroundings. After a four hour trip we stopped. We had arrived in Sepsiszentgyorgy (Saintgeorge), in the Kovaszna district. Here they had us get off the truck and in the morning took us to a forced-labor camp at rifle-point. From early 4:00 am till late at night we cleaned the pastures. Later they put us in a glass factory to work. We could speak to no one. Armed guards followed us everywhere. If we dared to speak to one another or question the guards we were beaten. I had expected to be taken much farther then this, therefore I ask the neighbor to take my daughter and the nanny to my parents to Besenyo. For five years we did not see her or hear about her. Letters were forbidden. No one knew of our whereabouts or whether we were even alive. Six months later we were again taken in the night. This time to Dobrugea, Macin county. We went by freight trucks to the Danube River. From there we continued by boat to Puiernitza. A thorny, burned-out area where not even grass grew. Here was our prison: long, low wooden buildings, each housing 35 of us prisoners. We each had a bed and a blanket, nothing more. We stood in line for our food: a small bowl of soup, barely enough to keep us from dying of starvation. The guards who pointed their weapons at us were Romanian communists. We were alternately called "homeless"= "bozgor" or "capitalist Hungarians"= "burzsuly". We were apparently guilty on two counts: that we were not communists and that we were Hungarians. In the morning we would stand in line to receive our work orders for the day. I was assigned to care for 13 cows: to clean their stalls; to feed them 3 times daily (their food was brought in by boat); to milk them 3 times daily. This was an enormous task for a women.

One night they took my husband in shackles, no one knew his destination. Only after five years I learned that he had been imprisoned near Bicaz, manpower was needed for the construction of the water power for electricity of the country. Here he was held with murderers and other criminals, forced to work in striped prison garb. When he became ill and could not work fast enough he was beaten. Therefore he began a hunger strike, so they would take him in front of the officials to be informed on what charge he was being held prisoner. This was met with no result. It took my husband four and a half long years to get his wish to stand before a court of justice. By this time he was so ill that they had no use for him; he could no longer work. He was then charged with being an enemy of the communist system and he didn't "deserve" freedom. (It was just in this way that his brother died in prison at the young age).

To continue with my story, I cut my finger and developed blood poisoning. Finally they took me to Braila, a port city,where the hospital was. The guard wanted to take me back on that day but the doctor did not agree. In one week I recovered. Four and a half year past by this way. I knew nothing of my husband or my baby daughter. Each night I prayed that I would live to see them once more. In order to ease my burden, to survive the hard work and the long hours, I named each cow after family members and close friends. I named the smallest and the youngest one after my daughter Ildiko, the oldest one after once mine but now my daughter's nanny Ida Mama. My husband was released in 1954. He was given a train ticket to his brother's place where he was reunited with our daughter. She did not recognize her own father. That evening they knelt together thanking God for his release and begging for my freedom.

During the summer vacation my husband brought her to visit me. She did not remember me. Ildiko was allowed to stay one month. Each day I brought her a small cup of milk under my apron so the guards would not notice, for it was forbidden. The month passed quickly. It was dangerous for her to stay longer. I feared they would keep her to work as a prisoner. Our separation was terribly difficult. My husband at 46 was completely white-haired, ill and very weak. He wrestled with my little girl who would not tear herself from me. The boat was ready to go, he finally unbuckled his leather belt and with that strapped her to the boat's mast. She fought with fantastic strength like she would fight for her life. The boat was on its way and despite the engines noise and the churning water we could hear her cries for a long time: "Mother, Mother". Even the guard, my escort to the shore, turned his head away to suppress his emotions.

In another six months I was released. My release was due I believe, to the many individual letters and requests for my freedom sent to the capitol from our town Ajta. They gave evidence and assurances that we were innocents and we helped everyone who needed help. Many of them are still there, although no longer prisoners, they have no where to go and being older can not adjust to the communist society.

On my release I also went first to my brother-in-law's home where my daughter resided at that time. They had also experienced much hardship and persecution. All their lands and livestock were taking from them, they were fortunate to have the roof over their heads. Later we rented a room. The three of us and the nanny Ida lived in a tiny room; the table served as a bed at night for my daughter. Most weeks we received packages by train with food without a return address. We knew the people from Ajta were helping us. My husband found a job in another city, they knew he was in prison, but hired him because they knew he was innocent.

Since then we returned secretly to our home in Ajta only once. The "collective"(Agricultural Association), had moved into our home as their official's residence. The land is idle and uncultivated. When I tried to enroll my daughter into the high school in Kovaszna they would not accept her because they claimed she was an "exploiter". We succeed to enroll her far away near Brasso where the director overlooked the "exploiter" children's status.

I swear before God, that what I have written here is the truth.

With God's help, I arrived safely yesterday November 16, 1988 at 5:00 pm to the United States of America to finally breath the air of freedom. At 74 years of age I have succeeded in reaching the land of the free; a land my husband did not live to see. He died a few months ago.

I don't know as yet what I'll find in America; its appearance, be it rich or poor, the kind of people who live here? I know that this is a free country and the destructive power of communism cannot reach here. Thank you for accepting me.

God bless America !

Taylor, November 17, 1988
Korina Szombathy

Translated by: Melinda Nagy-Garcia

Korina on her way to the Hungarian-American Reformed Church.

FACTS FOR THE READER

(About Transylvania's History)

Transylvania "The Land Beyond the Forests" is located in eastern central Europe, had been the integral part of the Hungarian Kingdom from 1000 until 1921, and is the citadel of Hungarian culture in the Carpathian Basin. At the end of World War I, as part of the Treaty of Trianon in 1920 the Allies annexed Transylvania from Hungary to Romania. The people who lives in Transylvania called "Szekely" belong to the Hungarians, speak the Hungarian language from the Finno – Ugric language family and share the same culture. They are regarded as the oldest core of Hungarians in Transylvania. Descendants of Attila the Hun "The Scourge of God "who arrived with his troops in Transylvania around the fifth Century AD. The Szekelys are known to be strong-willed, hard-working, resourceful people who are temperamental, full of virtue and have a good sense of humor. They are honest, trustworthy and passionate people who are very proud of their heritage.

The Early History of Transylvania

500BC-1000AD

5th Century BC	Transylvania settled by Agathyrsi with the Dacians
120 – 270 AD	150 years of Roman occupation
270 – 420	First wave of the Great Migration, gots, visigots...
380 - 400	The Huns (Hungarians) moved in
	The new power of the Huns installed
6th – 7th Century	After the disintegration of Attila the Hun's Empire various migrants moved in: avars, gepids, slavs, bulgars ….
	The Avars took over the Gepids and ruled
9th Century	Bulgarian Empire established
862	Hungarians entered Transylvania to overthrow the Bulgar rule in the principality of Great Moravia.
896	Magyar leader Arpad led Hungarians into the Carpathian Basin.
1000	Transylvania became Hungarian province Beginning of Christianity enforced by King Stephen of Hungary

Medieval History of Transylvania

1000 - 1900

10th Century	The Carpathian Basin was populated by Szekelys (Transylvanians) under the lead of King Stephen who was called "The Saint King".
1200	Gesta Hungarorum (Deed of Hungarians)
1222	King Andrew II estates of Szekelys and Wallahians
	First appearance of Vlachs or Wallachians from Balcan Mountains recruited by the Byzantine army launching attach on Hungary. Fact mentioned by a Byzantine chronicler.
	Under King Andrew II a number of semi nomadic shepherds called Vlachs or Wallachians, ancestors of Romanians, settled in Transylvania.
1241	Mongol armies attacked Transylvania but were defeated.
1366	Romanians removed from power
1440	John Hunyadi rules, father of the Hungarian King Matthias Corvin voivod of Transylvania
1526	Battle of Mohacs, the main Hungarian army and King Louis II slain
1600	Michael the Brave tried to unite three principalities: Wallachia, Moldova and Transylvania, did not succeed.
1613	Autonomous - Transylvania's Golden Age under Gabriel Bethlen and Rakoczi Mutual

	tolerance of the religions: Roman Catholics, Calvinists, Lutherans and Unitarians.
1683 - 1918	Austro-Hungarian Empire under Austrian rule
1683	Defeat of the Ottomans with Habsburg's help
1711	Austrian control over Transylvania
1848	Warfare erupted for Hungarian independence
	Sandor Petofi hero/poet wrote and recited the "Nemzeti Dal" (National Song), killed at a young age during the Revolution.
	General Jozef Bem had ousted the Austrians from Transylvania.
1849	Austrian Emperor Franz Joseph appealed to Russian troops.
April 19,1849	The Hungarian Revolution leader Kossuth Lajos became governor of Hungary for a short period of time.
August 9, 1849	Battle of Temesvar in Transylvania, Bem's army was defeated.
	The Execution Order signed by the Austrian general Haynau
October 6, 1849	Execution of the thirteen Hungarian generals in Arad, Transylvania called "Martyrs of Arad".
October 6	Mourning Day for the Hungarian nation
1867	Austro-Hungarian Emperor established, Hungary became providence of Austria.

Modern History of Transylvania

1900 – Present

1914	The first World War begins
1914	The Romanian King Carol refused to join the First World War.
1916	Romania joined the Triple Entente by signing the Military Convention with the Entente which reorganizes Romania's rights over Transylvania.
1920	Treaty of Trianon awarded Transylvania to Romania, defines the borders between Hungary and Transylvania.
1944	Soviet Military Administration stops the bloodshed against ethnic Hungarian civilians by the Romanian troops.
1944	Second World War starts, at the end of the war communism installs.
1948-49	Confiscation of the citizens properties 80% - 100% houses, fields, forests and meadows. Deportation of the Hungarian noble families from Transylvania to hard labor camps and jails.
1952 – 1968	Creation of the Hungarian Autonomous Province inhabited by a compact population of Szekely Hungarians.
	Total population: Hungarians 77.3%, Romanians 20.1%, Gypsies 1.5%, Germans 0.4%, Jews 0.4%, official language Romanian.

1956	Hungarian Revolution for Freedom against Soviet union
October 22, 1956	Students in Budapest demanding withdrawal of Soviet troops, democracy, celebration of Hungarian holidays and removal of the Stalin statue. Secret police joined with Russian tanks opened fire at the demonstrators. Peaceful march became massacre. This National War freed Hungary for five days when Khrushchev the Soviet President with the Russian tanks made Hungary silent.

A little Hungarian story from 1956

A small boy rings the doorbell of a house and an old lady opens the door. "What do you want, little one?", she asks.

Small boy: May I come in please?"

Old lady: "Come in little boy, but wipe your feet properly". The boy wipes his feet, enters and asks: "Lady, please may I shoot from your window?"

1960	Two million Hungarians lived in Transylvania, out of ten some million in the entire country of Romania. The Romanian government eliminated the Hungarian Autonomous Province, for romanization purposes.
1965 – 1989	Nicolae Ceausescu and Elena his wife dominated over Transylvania and Romania.

	Human rights were brutally suppressed, great hardship period, nationalism, repression of the large Hungarian minority in Transylvania.
1980	The Ceausescu regime resettled some Hungarians to other parts of the country for merging purposes. No Hungarian color displays allowed, the National Anthem banned, censorship of the Hungarian newspapers, many Hungarian schools closed, restriction of Hungarian language.
1989	Temesvar – the Hungarians in Transylvania formed a human shield around the home of the human rights militant Reverend Laszlo Tokes to prevent the Secret Service arresting him.
December 25, 1989	Revolution against the Ceausescu regime in Transylvania and Romania.
	Ceausescu and his wife were tried by a military tribunal and shot.
	Communism ended. Unfortunately, the fall of communism has not improved the Human Rights conditions for the Hungarians in Transylvania.

Transylvanian Anthem

Written by: Csanady Gyorgy in 1921
Translated by: Melinda Nagy-Garcia

Who knows where, where destiny will lead us,
On rough roads and throughout the dark nights.
Lead your people to victory once more,
Prince Csaba, on his star paved path.

Handful of Szekelys crumbling into pieces,
Among the roaring battles of many nations,
Hundreds of times their waves submerge us,
Don't let us lose Transylvania, our Lord!

Hungarian National Anthem

Written by: Ferenc Kolcsey 1823
Translated by: Bela Berde Jr.

God bless the Hungarians
With grace, wealth and high spirits,
Extend toward them Your protective arms
When they battle with the enemy.
Who harmful destiny tore apart,
Bring onto them cheerful years,
This nation endured enough
For the past and for the future.

ABOUT THE AUTHOR

Ildiko Eva Szombathy's wishes came true, arriving with her son Bela Jr. and daughter Melinda to the free land of the United States of America. She found work in a Hungarian pastry shop and in a hotel where little language knowledge was required. To make ends meet, in her spare time she interpreted Romanian and Hungarian languages for Language Center International and Executive Language Services, Incorporated. She also taught Hungarian language for Speak Easy and Gamboa Language Schools. A few years later, she enrolled in college courses to earn her degree in nursing.

"In your careers, you will meet many people. All are significant. They deserve your attention and care, even if all you do is smile and say hello."

—Joanna C. Jones

Working as a healthcare provider for close to twenty years, Ildiko helps people day by day as she promised to God when Bela Jr. fought his battle with cancer. She is a happy grandmother of three: Viktoria, Kristina, Jaime Jr. and feels safe and privileged to live in America, enjoying the various benefits of freedom that never should be taken for granted.

With strong beliefs, perseverance, and knowledge, DREAMS COME TRUE!

From left to right: Kristina, Jaime Jr. and Viktoria.

THANK YOU NOTE

My children and I would like to extend our deepest gratitude to the government of the United States of America for accepting us into the light of freedom, furthermore for allowing us to start a new life, protecting us, and opening the doors of education.

We enjoy the freedom of speech and religion, and the notion of being respected as human beings.

It is an uplifting feeling to know that the following generations will not experience the cruelty of communism, and that they will live a free and peaceful life in the greatest and most powerful country in the world.

"God bless America, my home, sweet home."